* * * * * * * * * * * * * *

SPORTS CHEATS

* * * * * * * * * * * * * *

T0062041

→»—► By Virginia Loh-Hagan ◄—«←

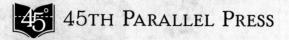

45TH PARALLEL PRESS

Published in the United States of America by Cherry Lake Publishing Group
Ann Arbor, Michigan
www.cherrylakepublishing.com

Reading Adviser: Beth Walker Gambro, MS, Ed., Reading Consultant, Yorkville, IL
Book Designer: Melinda Millward

Photo Credits: cover, title page: © Garsya/Shutterstock; page 7: © IMG Stock Studio/Shutterstock; page 9: © John Kropewnicki/
Shutterstock; page 11: © Georgios Tsichlis/Shutterstock; page 13: © Real Sports Photos/Shutterstock; page 15: © Perry Correll/
Shutterstock; page 16: © PeopleImages.com - Yuri A/Shutterstock; page 19: © Diego Barbieri/Shutterstock; page 20: © Vit
Kovalcik/Shutterstock; page 23: © FOTOKITA/Shutterstock; page 25: © Paul Yates/Shutterstock; page 27: © wavebreakmedia/
Shutterstock; page 29: © Sports Images/Dreamstime.com

Graphic Element Credits: Cover, multiple interior pages: © marekuliasz/Shutterstock,
© Andrey_Kuzmin/Shutterstock, © Here/Shutterstock

Copyright © 2024 by Cherry Lake Publishing Group
All rights reserved. No part of this book may be reproduced or utilized
in any form or by any means without written permission from the publisher.
45TH Parallel Press is an imprint of Cherry Lake Publishing Group.

Library of Congress Cataloging-in-Publication Data has been filed and is available at catalog.loc.gov.

Cherry Lake Publishing Group would like to acknowledge the work of the Partnership for 21st Century Learning,
a Network of Battelle for Kids. Please visit http://www.battelleforkids.org/networks/p21 for more information.

Printed in the United States of America
Corporate Graphics

About the Author

Dr. Virginia Loh-Hagan is an author and educator. She is currently the Director of the Asian Pacific Islander Desi American
(APIDA) Center at San Diego State University and the Co-Executive Director of The Asian American Education Project. She lives
in San Diego with her very tall husband and very naughty dogs.

Note from publisher: Websites change regularly, and their future contents are outside of our control.
Supervise children when conducting any recommended online searches for extended learning opportunities.

TABLE OF CONTENTS

* * * * * * * * * * * * * *

* * * * * * * * * * *
INTRODUCTION
* * * * * * * * * * *

Imagine winning a game. Only you didn't really win. You cheated. You didn't play fairly. You lied. You were dishonest. How would you feel? Is cheating worth it?

Sports are contests. They're games. Players have skills. They practice. They work hard. They compete against others. They test their talents. They want to be the best. Many sports players are heroes. They're loved.

But some **athletes** cheat. Athletes are people who play sports. There are different ways of cheating. Cheating upsets fans. Fans love watching sports. But they hate cheaters. Players are disgraced. They're booed. They ruin the fun of games. Learn about famous sports cheats in history.

* * * * * * * * * * *
CURRENT CASE:

Say Nope to Dope!

* * * * * * * * * * *

Sports test people's limits. Some athletes push those limits. They may dope. Doping means taking banned drugs. These drugs enhance performance. They make athletes stronger. They make them faster. They give them an unfair edge. Doping is cheating. It's not natural. It's also against the rules. Some athletes who dope get caught. They get punished.

Lance Armstrong (born 1971) is a cyclist. He won many bike races. He was accused of doping. Many of his awards were taken away. In 2014, Russian athletes were in the Winter Olympics. They won the most medals. But many had doped. Their medals were taken away. They were banned. They couldn't play in future games. Athletes who dope fall in status. They become known as cheaters. They lose many fans.

* * * * * * * * * * * *
NERO,
SELF-DECLARED OLYMPIC CHAMPION (67)
* * * * * * * * * * * *

Olympia is in Greece. The Olympic Games started there. Only Greek people could compete. But Nero (37–68) ignored this rule. Nero was an ancient Roman emperor. He was cruel. He broke many rules. The Olympics were every 4 years. Nero made them move it. He wanted to be in the games. Nero made Greece hold the games later. He would be in Greece for them. The games took place in 67.

Nero **bribed** judges. To bribe is to pay someone to break a rule or law. He added musical events. He added poetry readings. These were things he liked to do. He competed in the **chariot** race. Chariots are carts. They have 2 wheels. Four horses pull them. But Nero used 10 horses. He fell out. He didn't finish the race. The judges still gave him first prize. He gained many top prizes. After he died, he was removed from the champion list.

Zeus is the king of all Greek gods. Ancient Greek athletes stood before his statue. They vowed not to cheat.

* * * * * * * * * * *

A BOAT RACE,
THE FIRST COLLEGE CHEATING SCANDAL (1852)

* * * * * * * * * * * *

A boat race took place in 1852. It was the first U.S. college sporting event. Harvard and Yale are top colleges. They competed against each other. The race was at Lake Winnipesaukee. This lake is in New Hampshire. One thousand people came.

Railroad companies funded the race. They wanted people to attend. They wanted to promote their businesses. They gave students money. They paid travel costs.

Harvard cheated. Their **coxswain** wasn't a student. A coxswain steers the boat. Other team members weren't students. They were professional rowers. They were hired to compete. This was against the rules.

Harvard won. The cheating was found out much later. Nothing was done. The race was popular. They started having it every year starting in 1859. It is still held today.

This boat race still takes place today. It has changed locations.

SPYRIDON BELOKAS, MARATHON CHEATER (1896)

Spyridon Belokas (1877–unknown) was a Greek athlete. He competed at the 1896 Summer Olympics. He ran the **marathon**. Marathons are footraces. They're long-distance. They're about 26 miles (42 kilometers).

Seventeen athletes ran the Olympic marathon. Belokas was one. He crossed the finish line. He was in third place. He was behind 2 other Greek runners.

But Belokas cheated. He didn't run the whole way. He rode a horse and carriage. He did this for part of the course. He was **disqualified**. This means he was kicked out. Another runner took third place instead. Belokas's actions hurt Greece.

Athens is in Greece. It hosted the first modern Olympic Games in 1896.

Case Four

****

MADELINE AND MARGARET DE JESUS, SWITCHED (1984)

****

The 1984 Olympics were in Los Angeles. Los Angeles is in California.

Madeline de Jesus (born 1957) competed in track and field. This includes running, jumping, and throwing. She represented Puerto Rico. She competed in the long jump. She competed as a **sprinter**. Sprinters run fast. They run short distances.

Madeline did the long jump first. She hurt her leg muscle. She knew she couldn't sprint later. She talked to her sister. Her sister is Margaret de Jesus (born

1957). Margaret was in the crowd. They're twins. They look the same. Margaret took Madeline's place. But they were caught. The coach kicked them out.

Sprinters run fast over short distances. Madeline de Jesus hurt her leg and knew she couldn't sprint.

PHILIPPINES LITTLE LEAGUE,
PLAYER ISSUES (1992)

Kids play baseball. They play in the Little League. They have a World Series. The World Series is a championship game.

The Philippines are in Southeast Asia. They have a Little League team. They played in the 1992 World Series. They played against the Long Beach team. Long Beach is in California.

The Filipino team won. They became international champions. But they cheated. They broke rules about age. Some players were too old. Players cannot be older

The Little League hosts a World Series every year.

The Filipino team ultimately had to give up
their Little League World Series title.

than 12. The Filipino team also broke **residency** rules.
Residency is where one lives. Some players lived
outside the area.

The Filipino team had to give up the title. Long Beach
became the champions.

COLD CASE:

The Unsolved Mystery of the Black Sox Scandal

The Black Sox Scandal was a baseball scandal. It was also called the "Big Fix." It happened at the 1919 World Series. People bet on the game. The Chicago White Sox were a popular team. They had won 88 games. They were favored to win. The White Sox lost. Eight players were accused of cheating.

The players went to court. Four confessed to a grand jury. They said they lost on purpose. They said they took bribes. The case went to trial. Evidence went missing. The confessions were gone. The players were found not guilty.

But they were called the "Black Sox." They were banned from playing. They were banned from getting awards.

The truth is unknown. Stories changed. Fans debated. No one really knows.

TONYA HARDING,
ICE COLD SCANDAL (1994)

Tonya Harding (born 1970) was an ice skater. So was Nancy Kerrigan (born 1969). They competed against each other. They were **rivals**. Rivals are people who compete for the same prize.

In 1994, Kerrigan was practicing. She was at an ice rink. A man attacked her. He had a club. He struck her right knee. Kerrigan cried out in pain. Her leg was bruised. She had to stop competing. Harding won the 1994 U.S. championship.

Kerrigan was at the ice rink to practice.
She didn't expect to get attacked.

Tonya Harding won the 1994 U.S. championship. This was after Nancy Kerrigan dropped out because of her knee injury.

Harding's husband and bodyguard had ordered the **hit**. A hit is a planned attack. Harding denied being involved. It seemed like she tried to get Kerrigan out of the way. She later said she "knew something was up."

WORST-CASE SCENARIO:

Lying in the Paralympics

* * * * * * * * * * *

The Paralympic Games are special. They're sports contests. They're for disabled athletes. They take place after the Olympics. In 2000, they were held in Sydney. Sydney is in Australia. Spain's basketball team played. They won. Carlos Ribagorda was on the team. He was also a reporter. He was working undercover. Ribagorda said most of his teammates weren't disabled. He said they were faking. He said they had fake papers. He said no tests were done. He blamed the Spanish Federation of Sports for People with Intellectual Disabilities (FEDDI). He said the organization wanted to win medals. He said they wanted to gain more sponsorships. There was an investigation. Ten of the 12 players weren't disabled. The team was banned. They had to return their gold medals.

HOLYFIELD VS. TYSON,
AN EARFUL (1997)

Mike Tyson (born 1966) is a boxer. Evander Holyfield (born 1962) is also a boxer. Both are champions. They were rivals. They had 2 major boxing matches.

"The Bite Fight" is famous. It took place in 1997. It took place in Las Vegas. Las Vegas is in Nevada. Holyfield was winning. Tyson didn't like that. He bit part of Holyfield's ear. He tore it off. He spit it out. He did this in the third round. Holyfield was bleeding. But they kept boxing. Tyson tried to bite him again. The match ended.

Tyson was disqualified. He was fined. He lost his boxing **License**. A license is a permit. It allows you to do something. But Tyson and Holyfield later became friends.

The Holyfield vs. Tyson fight was called "The Sound and the Fury." It made a lot of money.

* * * * * * * * * *
TIM DONAGHY, NBA REFEREE BETTING SCAM
(2007)
* * * * * * * * * *

Referees are like judges. They decide fouls. They decide scores. They ensure fairness. But some make mistakes. Some even cheat.

In 2007, there was a scandal. NBA stands for National Basketball Association. Tim Donaghy (born 1967) was an NBA referee. He bet on games. He gave tips to friends. He shared information about players. He made unfair calls. He **fixed** games. Fix means to arrange who will win.

Donaghy did this for 4 seasons. He made money. He worked with organized crime members. He made them money. He was caught. He went to jail. Many people were upset with him. He dishonored the game.

Tim Donaghy said he "brought shame on myself, my family and the profession."

TOM WILLIAMS,
BLOODGATE (2009)

Rugby is a team sport. It's like American football. Players run. They hold the ball.

The Harlequins are an English team. Leinster is an Irish team. They played each other in 2009. Tom Williams (born 1983) played for the Harlequins. Dean Richards (born 1963) was the Harlequins' coach.

Williams was playing. The scores were close. Richards wanted to put in a more experienced player. He told

Williams to fake an injury. Williams used a fake blood pill. He acted like he was hurt. Richards and Williams were caught. They were punished. They were banned. They were fined. Richards lost his job.

One way to score a point in rugby is called a try.
A try is scored when a player touches the ball to
the ground in the in-goal area of the opposite team.

* * * * * * * * * * *

TOM BRADY,
FLAT FOOTBALLS (2015)

* * * * * * * * * * *

Tom Brady (born 1977) was an NFL player. NFL means National Football League. He was captain of the New England Patriots. In 2014, the Patriots played the Indianapolis Colts. The game would decide who went to the Super Bowl. The Patriots won.

But Brady was accused of cheating. He was accused of ordering the **deflation** of footballs. Deflation means to release air. This results in flat balls. This scandal was called "Deflategate." Flat balls are easier to catch. They are easier to hold onto. They do not bounce as far.

Brady was punished. He couldn't play in 4 games. The Patriots had to pay $1 million. Brady denies any wrongdoing. He said, "I didn't alter the balls in any way."

Tom Brady claims he didn't order the deflation of footballs.

FOR YOUR EYES ONLY...
* * * * * * * * * *
HOW TO BE A SPORTS CHEAT!*

Do you want to be a sports cheat? Do you have what it takes? Here are 3 tips:

Tip #1: Know the sport.
Learn the rules. Know how to play. Know how to score. Know what happens when rules are broken. Study the sport's history. You can't cheat what you don't know.

Tip #2: Know the shortcuts.
Shortcuts are quicker ways to do things. Look for different ways to win. Look for ways to get around the rules. Look for tricks.

Tip #3: Don't get caught.
Winning is public. You'll get attention. Don't leave behind proof. Get people to support you.

*WARNING: Cheaters can lose a lot more than a game. Play your best. Play fair. Don't be a sports cheat.

ICYW: IN CASE YOU'RE WONDERING...

The Science Behind Cheating

* * * * * * * * * * *

Why do athletes cheat? Sports are competitive. It's stressful. It's all about winning. There are limited numbers of winners. The stakes are high. Being the best brings money. It brings fame. To some, cheating may be worth it. Also, teams can make cheating seem okay. Teams work together. They form strong bonds. They have a common goal. Shared rewards offer the highest cheating levels. Team members may justify cheating. But watching others cheat is different. That upsets people. People judge cheaters. They don't want to be like them.

GLOSSARY

athletes (ATH-leets) people who are skilled in sports

bribed (BRYEBD) paid someone to break a rule or law

chariot (CHEHR-ee-uht) a two-wheeled horse-drawn vehicle used in ancient warfare and racing

coxswain (KAHK-suhn) the steersman of a racing boat

deflation (dih-FLAY-shuhn) the action or process of letting air or gas out

disqualified (dis-KWAH-luh-fyed) declared ineligible because of an offense or violation

fixed (FIKST) changed a game's outcome by cheating

hit (HIT) a planned attack

license (LYE-suhns) a permit from an authority to own or use something, do a particular thing, or carry on a trade

marathon (MAHR-uh-thon) a long-distance running race of about 26 miles (42 km)

residency (REH-zuh-duhn-see) the place where someone officially lives

rivals (RYE-vuhlz) people who compete against each other for the same prize or goal

rugby (RUHG-bee) a game played with an oval ball that may be kicked, carried, and passed from hand to hand

shortcuts (SHORT-kuhts) shorter, quicker, alternative ways of doing or achieving something

sprinter (SPRIN-tuhr) a person who runs a short, fast race over the crossbar of the opponents' goal

LEARN MORE!

Editors of Sports Illustrated Kids. *All-Star Sports Trivia*. New York, NY: Sports Illustrated Kids, 2021

Editors of Sports Illustrated Kids. *The United States of Sports*. New York, NY: Sports Illustrated Kids, 2018.

Gitlin, Martin. *The Big Game*. Ann Arbor, MI: 45th Parallel Press, 2023

Gitlin, Martin. *Underdogs: Sports Champions*. Ann Arbor, MI: 45th Parallel Press, 2024

INDEX